A BED WITH MY NAME ON IT

Poems by

NINA BELÉN ROBINS

Thompson & Columbus, Inc., Publishers
New York

DEDICATED TO GTE

Without staff and teachers adopting me over the years,
I would have never come out alive. When my own parents
couldn't be there, she stepped in. The third parent. Still.

It hasn't changed.

NOTE

I have tried to recreate events, locales and conversations from my memories of them. In order to maintain their anonymity, in some instances I have changed the names of individuals and places, I may have changed some identifying characteristics and details such as physical properties, occupations and places of residence.

CONTENTS

A BED WITH
MY NAME
ON IT

PROLOGUE

The start

BEGINNINGS

You couldn't tell, when I smiled,
that front doors broke down,
punctured by shrieks,
or that the hole in the French doors
let the sunlight into the foyer,
there was water on the floor
of the bathroom.
Waves of fury trying to flood the house out.

Or that my sister
spent most days with her friends
to avoid becoming as fractured
as the paint on the slammed door.

My mother
salting the shower water.
(Tears hidden by the stream,
cries hidden by the stream,
curses hidden by the stream.
A fogged mirror, window).

If I smiled,
with crooked teeth,
giggled,
8-years-old,
(what damage can 8-year-olds
do, anyway.)

There were no scars,
no soap in my mouth,
talk-doctors,
skin etched expiration date,
amber alert
waiting in the night-light.

Just a girl,
two braids,
a loving mother and father,
a sister,
roller blades,
piano lessons,
vacations.

Everyone's question:

I wonder if that family knows
How lucky they are.

THE POEMS

What happened

BRIAN

Brian went off his meds again.
He remembered his purpose in life
is to kill all the devils in the world,
and his mom got scared,
called the cops,
now he's in the next room over
screaming about devils,
how we're all reincarnations of dinosaurs,
I walk over and introduce myself
and he smiles.

Brian never had a sister,
and I am a 12 year old innocent,
two days out of the emergency room,
(it takes that long to get settled;
the first night they wake you at 3 am to test for drugs
the first day is a dreamland)
and I listen, and laugh,
so he adopts me.

Brian is refusing the Thorazine,
even though he's seeing dinosaurs everywhere.
You know you're a reincarnated Velociraptor right?
You are smart and vicious and indestructible.
You're like the sister I never had.
He smiles, and I go back into my room and think,
Brian sees me for what I really am.

Brian is in the quiet room.
I passed by the door
and his bloody hand was hanging through the
six-inch by six-inch window,
and he looked out at me
half doped up on sedatives

just staring—
and I waved and smiled like I always do.

They shot Brian up with Thorazine
a whole week,
the mattress on the floor soaked in his urine.
But he's calmed down now,
they've got him on his doses
and we sit on the couch and watch Thundercats.

And he looks at me during the commercial and says,
Promise me you'll always take your meds.

JULIE

Julie's laugh kept her stories fiction.
How it'd bubble over coffee, dinner,

her smile unshaken, sturdy—
despite the whirlwind of stories behind her teeth.

I'd listen to her ventures through the calm of sushi,
then she'd leave me behind to jump the stars.

She told me about the mushrooms, first.
The visions in her room, the discovery of magic,

the freeing of the parties late at night—
the beauty of sunrise on ecstasy.

She'd confess escapades from the weekend before,
and then she'd laugh it off and pay the bill.

I'd wait in my sober ready to catch her,
she'd bounce from wild into my arms and back.

I stayed her safety net until
my sobriety became a white fence she no longer felt like crossing.

My mowed lawn and daisies
losing their appeal.

I last saw her in a series of pictures,
glazed, and half naked in a bar somewhere.

The first time her laugh and life
were in the same frame.

I don't know when her stories wrote the rest of her.
I feel like it was always hidden by her bellow.

That bubbling giggle, on Tuesday nights,
the only version of her I acknowledged.

Sipping my coffee unaware
how easily she was slipping away through teeth.

MOTHERS

I bet you never knew
half of us
cheek our meds,
but that's what my friend's
been doing for six months
and they can't tell.

The doctors?
They think the meds are working,
not that her mom
saw crazy everywhere
and my friend got in the way.

She's been cheeking her meds,
and I'm a little jealous.
They've been raising mine.
My med cup looks like Skittles,
but when I miss them
my brain catches fire
and the room swallows me,
so I take them.

You're either here because
you're crazy,
or because your parents are.
Sometimes both.
In the system
if you can't live at home,
you can't live at home.

We're all here checking in
every half hour,
sneaking cigarettes,
blowing the smoke through the fan.

She goes home on the weekends,
sleeps with her boyfriend.
Doesn't take her meds.

I missed mine yesterday
and the room spit me out into the sunrise.
Late night shows
not a lullaby.

If your parents are crazy
or you are,
it doesn't matter.
They just throw us all together.

Take your meds, girls.
Take your meds and go to sleep.

MALE STAFF

The first time I realized
authority was seducible
I took the sex-poem back.
The one I passed around
like cleavage,
my knee high boots.

Printed on the classroom computer,
a guessing game
at which teacher
would wear their excitement
so I could see.

I took it back,
attached it to a string to dangle.
Catching older men
like open-mouthed fish.

This one put a pillow on his lap.
This one memorized it.
This one promised to
email once I graduated.

My first lover,
the legal one,
the one I could strip for
without pretending it was accidental,
was older
like they were.

It didn't seem unusual
he wanted someone young.

This is what older men do.

The ones you tease
to premature measures.
The ones you torment.

You, *the fantasy.*

He used to tell me,
Even on thanksgiving
we want young, fresh turkeys.

I'd side-ponytail my hair,
put on a plaid skirt,
open up my legs.

Success
at last.

BANGS

The day we cut my bangs,
one did weed,
one did coke,
one did vodka,
and I was manic.

In the institution
they pretended
to notice your sniffle
or red eyes.
I was taking the meds
so it was no one's fault.

We took scissors into the bathroom,
I didn't look in the mirror.
9 pm, bedtime in an hour,
last cigarette break coming up.

A cottage full of girls with
too much oomph
and not enough freedom,
but we had scissors and friendship.
I didn't mind being
the beautician's guinea pig.

Well, it came out terrible.
They went from behind my ears,
curving up and down.

I think it was just a few months
before the boy got murdered,
the breakup
that left me bedridden,
before those girls
graduated and left me behind.

In the system,
you hold onto every fun day
with shaking hands
and half a brain.

You can wake up the next morning
and someone's suffocated in a shopping bag,
overdosed on a stash of ibuprofen,
or there's blood in the shower,
maybe it's your own.

Hair grows back even if you
cut it all off on drugs
or chemicals.
We all smiled that night,
only half remembered when
I woke up the next morning
with a story to tell.
A haircut.
The simple giggle
we all craved.

OPERA

We're seeing La Bohème tonight,
all of us dressed up.
Curled my hair,
wore my prettiest dress.

They can hear you, on stage
at The Met.
It's the acoustics.

So don't even whisper!
our teacher tells us
every time we go but
always takes us to the
rehearsals just in case.

Tonight it's the real deal though.
All ten of us piling
into the van.

Orchestra Seats.
Manhattan's 1%
surrounding us.

The show ends and
the lead comes out
to roaring applause.

You're really hot!
I call out,

a young voice among
the seniors.
Rebellious etiquette.

So he misses his bow!

What girl is out there?
This vixen beauty at the opera.

Thirty minutes later
I'm knocked out
with my classmates
in the van.

Sucked back from the masses
to sedation
and curfew.

An opera singer
looking through the minglers,
wondering which
NYC Elite
called his name.

PING PONG

Over the ping pong table,
the heroin addict is just
the man who's restricted to pajamas
teaching you how to hit the ball.

You're twelve,
pretending you're Forrest Gump
with a butt injury,
not locked up in a unit
with the Chronics.

He's just the man with tattoos on his arm
who makes you promise not to do drugs,
and you hit the ball over the net
every day for two and a half weeks.

He'll sit on the couch with you,
your parents,
sometimes your sister.
Make you swear.
Never do this.

You do not notice the methadone pills
in his medicine cup
when you take your lithium,
the scars on his forearm.
They discharge you.
You forget.

You're sixteen
and they're all stoned on something.
You've forgotten the ping pong table, mostly,
the man with the tattoos.

They offer you,
smoke everywhere.
You say no.

Somewhere
a recovering addict
wins his match.

JOSIE

I came home to Josie rocking
back and forth
on the couch
overdosed on a bottle of Advil.

Came up the stairs
and they were keeping her
eyes open.

Talk to me Josie,
they kept saying.
You can't go to sleep now.

She always tried to get the ambulance
to come
and we'd joke about it.
She'd come up with any fake disease
and call 911.
We'd sit on her bed all night
and laugh and laugh.

A month ago
I saw her kissing my ex-boyfriend
on the mouth.
We'd only been split up a week.

I wished so hard she'd disappear.

I sat down on the couch
and held her hand.

Stay with us Josie,
the ambulance is coming.

I thought wishes never came true Josie.
Just keep your eyes open.
Don't leave us.
Please stay.

YVETTE

I'm the strongest girl in school,
so my staff Yvette's gotta be stronger.
Has to be 20
pounds ahead of me.
I can lift 165 pounds,
she's got me beat
At 185.

When my boyfriend and I broke
up she spied in the background.
I could take him
if he tried anything,
but she's stronger than me.
Just in case.

All year she's been charging me
two bucks for the cans of Coke
I get from her.
Last week I needed clothes
so she got an envelope from the closet.
Here, kid.
You're so damn thirsty all the time.

Even when I'm not cutting
I sleep on the couch downstairs.
Travel Channel and a bowl of oatmeal
stronger than the sedatives
the doctors give me.

I heard she gives hugs on graduation.
Heard she cares even though she claims
she doesn't.

No one tells me *shit isn't that deep*
as much as she does
but she still barges into my room
and checks for razors under the bed.
Knows all my hiding spots.

I trek across campus for her
and they tease me.
Yvette could ask me anything
I'd do it.

Your mother didn't choose you.
Mine either.
Birth lottery doesn't apply here.

My friends call me Meathead
because I'm stronger than all the boys.
Lift 30 pounds in each hand.
All 250 pounds of med weight
pushing through.

She says I've always been beautiful.
She's the only one strong enough
to push me down the snow drift
on the tube.

Gets a running start.
Pushes me down.
I spin around
and hers is the only
face I see as I fall
to the bottom.

RACHEL

Today is Rachel's last day,
and she grabbed me by the wrist
and kissed me as the door closed.

On the woman's unit,
we are woven together
full of estrogen
and no physical contact.
Rachel is just-out-of-the-closet
lonely and
I've been cooped up
in a group home
for the middle-aged
and it's not like I've *never*
crushed on a lady before.
So we kiss for a minute
when everyone is distracted.
She gets her bags,
the confiscated wallet,
phone, and they lock the door behind her.

Touch can be gift-wrapped
in any old paper.
If it's been awhile since it's been presented
it's not about the packaging.

The TV's buzzing in the common area,
the prodigy's banging on the piano,
I go to lunch,
try to forget she's out in the sunlight.
Eat my TV dinner,
count the days
until my own insurance runs out.
Stare at the pay phone.
Wonder if she'll call.

MONIQUE

Monique forgot she had
poured the boiling water
on her thigh,
so she did it again,
and we're sitting on the couch
in the hallway.

The shock therapy made me forget
so I'm back.

Sometimes the rhythm
of bed checks,
private showers,
quiet,
help to forget, also.

The hot food,
evening snack,
protective little universe
hidden behind the walls.

So she forgot.
Re-scalded
the skin off her leg.

Electric probes
waiting again for later.

Her kids
running the halls.
Mommy sitting on the couch
with her friends.

STRIP SEARCH

The last time I went inpatient
I didn't bring much.
My therapist called me in
from the streets
with a flushed, soaked face
to keep me safe for a week.

It was summer,
and the interns
from med schools
patrolled the units.

Textbooks in their lockers,
sections highlighted
in pink or yellow:
diagnoses and treatments.

These are the illnesses out there.
Go look through the hospitals.
See which ones you can name.

It took 30 minutes to
bring me upstairs.
The nurses followed by a crowd
of clipboards,
ties,
A-line skirts,
and heels
into the bathroom.

Take your clothes off please.

They didn't close their eyes
until I requested it.
This was the prized show:
the privilege of seeing
the bipolar case
in the nude.

The twenty-something-year-old
textbook chapter
from last week:
the manic nipple piercings,
the razor lines.

A caged disorder
presenting itself in its most natural form.
Lesson 32 from the summer,
case 234.

VERONICA

Veronica came out of the shelter
to live here a year before I did.
I've been giving her my pants
since I lost weight
and she's been baking me cakes.

We both shouldn't be eating them,
her neuropathy is so bad
the hand-me-downs
are always on the floor covered
in feces.

Let's go for Chinese food
she said yesterday,
but we had to come back
halfway there
because her diaper leaked.

She's here because
her husband
had a fist
that loved her face more
than he did.

Husband, to shelter, to halfway house,
to shit filled pants on the floor
and cakes in the fridge
because who cares about life, anyway.

They went together to visit her daughter,
stayed in the same hotel.

Had sex.
She said he didn't hit her.

If they shared the bed
he woke up in urine,
she woke up with memories
of eating knuckles.

Came back and said,
Old habits die hard.

I stepped over my old pants,
ate a piece of cake.
We sat on the couch
and I ignored the wet spot.
Put my head on her shoulder.
Held her hand.

BECKY

When Becky got molested behind the drug store
the house was filled with cops.
Staff held her hand while
she held her Barbie backpack—
tried to explain
what happened.
Geoff hugged her.
Everyone knows staff isn't supposed to hug you,

but he loved her like his own
so we forgave him.

Becky was almost 30.
When her sugar would drop
we'd sit her down
with orange juice,
remind her when to shower.
She'd put her weekly $25 SSI check
on prepaid debit cards—
proudly bring them home to show us.
A Barbie backpack full of useless plastic.

I wonder about the man behind a drug store
seeing a 28-year-old
with a Barbie backpack,
odorous and trembling,
with prepaid debit cards
denied at the register for being empty,
and what it felt like to make her cry.

When Becky got molested behind the drug store
Geoff hugged her
and the ambulance came and took her
to the hospital for a week
where she was safe.

LAUREN

Lauren is spending the weekend at her mother's.
She left home when her mother's
bones were too old to support anyone
other than her own frame.

This week is electrolysis week
where Lauren pays
20 dollars for 20 minutes
and then goes out to lunch.

This is every Saturday.
Weekly complaints to her mother
that we *still* aren't doing the dishes,
there's *still* lint in the dryer,
leaving out
that she stole my food again
because the meds make her so hungry
nothing is safe from her appetite.

Lauren is 50.
Remembers her boyfriend
from the psyche ward.

In college I wasn't crazy like this
just the pressure did me in.
Mother tells me
I'm wound up tighter than a clock.

A ticking too loud
for more than one afternoon a week.

Lauren talks about her mother
every day.
Still a mama's girl.

We worry when her back is turned
what will happen
when her mother expires.

Whenever my friends take pictures
of their newborns,
those first few minutes
before life kicks in,
I wonder if any of them picture themselves
80-years-old,
taking their 50-year-old daughters
out to get electrolysis.

Memorized conversations.
One day a week.

Praying for relief.

MADISON

I don't know what's wrong with Madison
but she doesn't say hi back
when I leave for work.
I think she peed in the floor.
It takes thirty minutes to walk
every morning.
I'm running late.
I'm the first cashier.
She's the closest thing to a friend I have here
but she doesn't even look at me.

I know about the pain meds in her
suitcase she keeps under her bed,
but she's been doing better.
She's out of the nursing home.
So maybe she's sleepwalking.

I say hi again but she just stands there in her urine.
It's just sleepwalking I think.
I tell them downstairs she peed on the floor, since
it's not that out of nowhere
with the population here.
They say they'll send maintenance.

I go to work.
Don't think about it again.

Six hours and two tired feet later
I come home to eat lunch and Madison is gone.

You saved her life staff tells me,
when you told us about the urine.

Guess the suitcase full of pain meds was emptier than I realized.

I go make some soup or something.
Take a nap.
Honestly, I don't remember.
All the days tend to mesh into one.

PILL BOTTLE

When I think too much
they take my brain from me.
Put it in a bottle.
Lock up my thoughts
with child protective caps,
monthly refills,
and warn me not to operate heavy machinery.

I give it to them willingly.
Crawl into sleepy.
I'm so tired, anyway.
My thoughts like to see how fast
they can reach illogical,
like it's a contest with the night before.
Compete for the latest fallacy
and how I'll fall for it.
How it'll consume me,
and I'll rattle around the room.

So they tie me up and bottle me.
Dress me in orange with a white cap
and watch me nod.

When that happens,
there are no thoughts at all.
Just a bed,
the window of a car,
sometimes a public bench.
A numbness.
A frustrating comfortable.

THE HOME

There are no dogs in our backyard,
just the bedbugs the new girl brought in from the shelter,
and the roaches from
hotdogs at 2 am while staff is sleeping
because Joan drooled in the tacos again.
We don't look forward to Taco Tuesday
like the mainstreamers,
and I bet they can watch TV after eleven
although staff let us see the lock code
last night when she mistook us for human.
Two of us have kids but they don't live here,
reverse empty nest syndrome,
piled into an eleven person house.
We divvy up the food bills
like we budget or something,
but Uncle Sam funds our powdered mashed potatoes.
They taste the same as the mainstreamers,
just we mass produce them and try to make sure
Joan doesn't drool this time,
that Denise washed her hands after the bathroom
like my mom taught me when I was young,
but Denise is 25.
I'm 21.
This has been a year and a half.
In a bank account I'm putting my paychecks
together to get out of here.
The white picket fence locking us in
from society
like we're grounded.
11 women trying to learn how to cook,
clean the bathroom,
socialize
with the mainstreamers.

You're just like everyone else
staff tells me,
you're no different.
Then hands me my medicine
and I walk upstairs
in a stupor
and fall asleep
like they expect me to.

ON LEAVING THE SYSTEM

That first night in my room,
alone without supervision,
I pulled back the shades,
and the dirty air conditioner
blew stinky air against my face and I was free.

I could sleep naked here,
and it wasn't like staff could walk in on me.
I could lock the door
from the inside.
It could stay locked all day and all night
and no one could come in.
They didn't do room checks like I was used to.

The night wasn't forbidden for once.
I could go to the 24 hour CVS
for instance,
if I was thirsty at 3am,
and no one could stop me.

I could dance, even, now.
I was 22 after all,
There was no curfew.
I could put on my mini skirt,
my heels,
and just go out to any bar.
This is the freedom I lusted after.

So 3 or 4 times I did.
The whole summer.
But the way I told people,
you'd think it was every Friday night
the way I bragged.

You'd think I was this unleashed monster;
this sultry wild experienced woman
who danced, got the guys,
stayed up with the constellations
with this freedom, social life and all.

But I was closer with the air conditioner,
mostly.
Sometimes I'd talk to boys on the phone
till almost sunrise.
But usually I kept my door locked from the inside,
and listened to music.

And sometimes
I'd miss supervision.
The company, you know?
That feeling of not being alone in the world
still with a bed with my name on it.

EPILOGUE

Ten years later

NEW LOVE

He jokes that the bed isn't big
enough for all of us anymore.
Everyone involved has gotten bigger.
There is a softness love brings
and the kittens have grown.

We are becoming
cozier
in the bed sheets,
and plan to buy a bigger bed

for the cats
so they have room on the mattress.

If you were to ask them
how they felt about their humans
spreading out in their clothes
they'd probably tell you
how easy it is to purr
into sleep
on a cushion.

Only Bean worries
when I go to the mirror
to tweeze my chin.
Tries to knock the tweezers
from my paws,
purring on my shoulder.

Wondering how mommy
will fit through doors properly
without her whiskers.

ACKNOWLEDGMENTS

I would like to acknowledge Jennifer Giordano Magriz
for being my case worker for the nine years I lived at the YWCA.
Every breakdown I had I could go to her office and she
would be able to calm me down and send me on my way again
so I could continue to grow and eventually move out.

New Love was originally published in *Germ* Magazine.

THE YWCA IN WHITE PLAINS
WAS MY HOME FOR NINE YEARS.

After a year and a half in a group home and witnessing what my future would have been if I never tried to get healthy, I gathered enough money together for rent and deposit and moved in.

The YWCA offers affordable housing for women in transition from tough situations — jail, group homes, abusive relationships, drug dependencies. They provide a room with a locked door, on-call caseworkers, a food pantry, a clothing donations room, rehab services, fresh vegetables, social activities, computer classes and employment programs — and community.

As I lived there, I learned to cope with my bipolar disorder in the real world, worked part-time in a supermarket so I could pay rent, and built a life for myself because I had the freedom to do so while still having a safe place to come home to at night.

If it hadn't been there, I might have been institutionalized indefinitely.

For every book I sell, I will donate $1.00 to the YWCA to try to give back to the residence that saved my life.

You can see more about the YWCA here:

http://www.ywcawpcw.org/

SUPER- MARKET DIARIES

Nina Belén Robins

"Mild-mannered grocery store employee by day, Nina Robins is a well-known performance poet who has twice performed at the National Poetry Slam. Her poetry has been described as "exceptionally appealing," "heartbreakingly honest," and "subversively deep for work so overtly entertaining."

—Taylor Mali, author of
What Teachers Make

available in paperback and ebook format from amazon.com

PRAISE FOR *SUPERMARKET DIARIES*

This magnificent volume of poetry is the author's first published book but surely not her last. With impeccable insight and a vivacious appreciation for the human condition, Robins takes us on a journey behind the supermarket check-out counter. She offers us a unique glimpse into the lives of the ordinary people who cross her path each day, using her incredible poetic talents to convince us of the extra-ordinary humanity of each of them, and by extension, of ourselves. I highly recommend this book! — *choirqueer*

Simple observations, expressed with great insight, wisdom and eloquence. — *Dan Couture*

In a variety of stories through the eyes of a creatively observant cashier, Nina's writing is sharp witted, emotional, and promises to be very memorable! — *Zadra*

This is *The Spoon River Anthology* of supermarkets: insightful poems about customers, staff and life behind the cash register, by an exciting young NYC poet. Can't wait for the next book! — *Lori Ubell*

Nina Belén Robins is a three-time National Slam Poet, and author of the book of poems, *Supermarket Diaries*. She spent much of her life in various institutions, but has finally broken free and lives with her boyfriend and cats, working in the bakery department of a supermarket. She writes whenever possible, and wants to help normalize and destigmatize mental illness as best she can.